"Unlocking Life's Secrets: Timeless Wisdom for Achieving True Success"

Preface

In the quest for success, we often find ourselves seeking guidance from various sources—books, mentors, and experiences. Yet, amidst the vast ocean of advice and strategies, it is the fundamental principles that truly guide us toward a meaningful and successful life. *"Unlocking Life's Secrets: Timeless Wisdom for Achieving True Success"* is designed to be your compass in this journey. It's not just about achieving wealth or status but about finding fulfilment, balance, and purpose.

This book is a compilation of essential life wisdoms that have stood the test of time. It draws from ancient philosophies, modern psychology, and the experiences of those who have navigated their paths to success with grace and resilience. Each chapter explores a crucial principle, offering practical insights and actionable steps to integrate these timeless lessons into your daily life.

As you embark on this journey through the pages of this book, I invite you to keep an open mind and a reflective heart. The wisdom within is not merely theoretical but is meant to be experienced and lived. May these insights inspire you to unlock your full potential and lead a life of true success.

Index

Chapter 1: The Power of Mindset

Chapter 2: Embracing Failure as a Stepping Stone

Chapter 3: The Art of Setting Meaningful Goals

Chapter 4: Building Strong Relationships

Chapter 5: Consistency: The Key to Long-Term Success

Chapter 6: The Art of Time Management

Chapter 7: The Power of Positive Thinking

Chapter 8: Mastering Financial Management

Chapter 9: Embracing Lifelong Learning

Chapter 10: Building Resilience and Overcoming Adversity

Chapter 1

The Power of Mindset

Introduction

Mindset is the fundamental lens through which we view the world, approach challenges, and interpret experiences. Our mindset influences how we respond to obstacles, how we handle setbacks, and how we grow from our experiences. This chapter delves into the concept of mindset, focusing on the distinction between a growth mindset and a fixed mindset, and provides practical strategies to cultivate a growth mindset to enhance personal and professional success.

1.1 Growth vs. Fixed Mindset

Fixed Mindset:

- **Definition:** A fixed mindset is the belief that abilities, intelligence, and talents are static and unchangeable. Individuals with a fixed mindset believe that their qualities are innate and not subject to improvement.

- **Characteristics:**
    - **Avoidance of Challenges:** Individuals with a fixed mindset may shy away from challenges, fearing failure or looking foolish.
    - **Effort as Futile:** They may see effort as a sign of inadequacy, believing that if you have to work hard, it means you're not naturally gifted.
    - **Response to Criticism:** Criticism is often seen as a personal attack rather than constructive feedback.
    - **Success of Others:** The success of others may be perceived as a threat or a reflection of their own inadequacies.

Growth Mindset:

- **Definition:** A growth mindset is the belief that abilities and intelligence can be developed through dedication, hard work, and learning. This mindset fosters a love of learning and resilience.

- **Characteristics:**
    - **Embrace Challenges:** Individuals with a growth mindset actively seek challenges and view them as opportunities for growth.
    - **Effort as a Path to Mastery:** They believe that effort and practice are essential for improvement and success.
    - **Learn from Criticism:** Criticism is welcomed as a valuable source of information for learning and improvement.
    - **Inspiration from Others:** They find inspiration in the success of others, viewing it as a source of learning and motivation.

1.2 Impact on Personal and Professional Life

Personal Life:

- **Self-Esteem:** A growth mindset contributes to higher self-esteem as individuals learn to value their efforts and growth over innate talent.
- **Resilience:** It fosters resilience, helping individuals bounce back from setbacks and view failures as learning opportunities.
- **Relationships:** A growth mindset enhances personal relationships by encouraging open communication, empathy, and the ability to handle conflicts constructively.

Professional Life:

- **Career Development:** In the workplace, a growth mindset leads to greater professional development as individuals are more likely to pursue learning opportunities, seek feedback, and adapt to new challenges.
- **Problem-Solving:** It enhances problem-solving abilities, as individuals approach problems with a mindset of finding solutions rather than feeling defeated.
- **Leadership:** Leaders with a growth mindset are more effective in motivating and developing their teams, fostering a culture of continuous learning and improvement.

1.3 Cultivating a Growth Mindset

Embrace Challenges:

- **Seek Out New Experiences:** Actively look for opportunities that push you out of your comfort zone. For example, take on projects at work that stretch your abilities or learn a new skill.
- **Frame Challenges Positively:** Reframe challenges as opportunities to grow. Instead of focusing on the difficulty, concentrate on what you can learn from the experience.

Learn from Criticism:

- **Request Feedback:** Actively seek constructive feedback from colleagues, mentors, or friends, and view it as a tool for improvement rather than a personal critique.
- **Reflect on Criticism:** Take time to reflect on the feedback you receive and consider how it can help you enhance your skills or approach.

Celebrate Effort:

- **Recognize Your Progress:** Regularly acknowledge and celebrate your efforts and progress, not just the end results. This reinforces the value of hard work and persistence.
- **Set Process-Oriented Goals:** Focus on goals related to the process and effort rather than just outcomes. For example, set goals to improve your skills or knowledge rather than just achieving a specific result.

1.4 Practical Exercises

Mindset Reflection Journal:

- **Purpose:** To help you understand how your mindset influences your behavior and outcomes.
- **Instructions:** Reflect on recent challenges you faced. Write about how your mindset affected your approach and the outcomes. Consider how adopting a growth mindset could have changed the situation.

Growth Mindset Affirmations:

- **Purpose:** To reinforce a growth mindset through positive affirmations.
- **Instructions:** Create a list of affirmations that promote a growth mindset, such as "I can improve through effort and learning" or "Challenges are opportunities to grow." Repeat these affirmations daily to reinforce positive thinking.

1.5 Summary and Key Takeaways

Summary of Concepts:

- **Mindset Matters:** Your mindset influences how you approach challenges, handle setbacks, and grow personally and professionally.
- **Growth vs. Fixed Mindset:** A growth mindset fosters resilience, learning, and development, while a fixed mindset limits potential and growth.
- **Cultivating Growth:** Embracing challenges, learning from criticism, and celebrating effort are key strategies to developing a growth mindset.

Key Takeaways:

1. **Adopt a Growth Mindset:** Embrace challenges and view failures as learning opportunities. Focus on continuous improvement and effort rather than innate talent.
2. **Seek Feedback:** Actively seek and reflect on constructive criticism to enhance your skills and approach.
3. **Celebrate Effort:** Recognize and celebrate your efforts and progress to reinforce a growth mindset and maintain motivation.

By applying these principles, you can transform your mindset, leading to increased success and fulfilment in both your personal and professional life.

Chapter 2

Embracing Failure as a Stepping Stone

Introduction

Failure is often perceived as a negative experience, but it holds immense value as a stepping stone toward success. This chapter explores how to embrace failure, learn from it, and use it as a powerful tool for growth. By shifting our perspective on failure, we can transform setbacks into opportunities for improvement and ultimately achieve our goals.

2.1 The Nature of Failure

Redefining Failure:

- **Failure as Feedback:** Rather than viewing failure as a defeat, consider it valuable feedback. Failure highlights areas for improvement and provides insights into what went wrong.

- **Failure as a Learning Tool:** Every failure contains lessons that can guide you toward better strategies and solutions. It's an essential part of the learning process.

Historical Examples:

- **Thomas Edison:** Known for his numerous unsuccessful attempts before inventing the light bulb, Edison famously said, "I have not failed. I've just found 10,000 ways that won't work."

- **J.K. Rowling:** Before the success of the Harry Potter series, Rowling faced numerous rejections from publishers. Her persistence and ability to learn from rejection ultimately led to worldwide success.

- **Steve Jobs:** Jobs was fired from Apple, the company he co-founded, only to return years later and lead it to unprecedented success with products like the iPhone and iPad.

2.2 Learning from Failure

Analyzing Mistakes:

- **Identify What Went Wrong:** Take time to analyze the factors that contributed to the failure. Was it a lack of planning, poor execution, or external factors?

- **Extract Lessons:** Determine the lessons learned from the experience. What can be done differently in the future to avoid similar pitfalls?

Adjusting Strategies:

- **Refine Your Approach:** Based on the lessons learned, adjust your strategies and plans. This might involve changing your methods, seeking additional resources, or acquiring new skills.

- **Iterate and Improve:** Use the feedback from failure to iteratively improve your approach. Continuous refinement based on past experiences leads to better outcomes.

2.3 The Role of Resilience

Building Resilience:

- **Develop Emotional Strength:** Resilience involves developing emotional strength to bounce back from setbacks. Techniques include mindfulness, stress management, and positive self-talk.

- **Cultivate a Support Network:** Surround yourself with supportive individuals who can provide encouragement and perspective during challenging times.

Maintaining Motivation:

- **Set Small Goals:** Break down larger goals into smaller, manageable tasks. Achieving these smaller goals can maintain motivation and provide a sense of progress.

- **Visualize Success:** Regularly visualize your long-term success to stay focused and motivated despite setbacks.

2.4 Practical Exercises

Failure Analysis Worksheet:

- **Purpose:** To systematically analyze recent failures and extract valuable lessons.

- **Instructions:** Create a worksheet with sections for describing the failure, identifying what went wrong, and listing lessons learned. Use this worksheet to reflect on recent failures and develop strategies for improvement.

Resilience Building Activities:

- **Mindfulness Practice:** Engage in mindfulness activities, such as meditation or deep breathing exercises, to enhance emotional resilience.

- **Support Network Engagement:** Regularly connect with your support network to share experiences, seek advice, and gain encouragement.

2.5 Summary and Key Takeaways

Summary of Concepts:

- **Failure as a Learning Tool:** Failure should be viewed as an opportunity for growth and learning rather than a setback.

- **Analyzing and Adjusting:** Systematically analyze failures to identify lessons and adjust your strategies accordingly.

- **Building Resilience:** Develop emotional resilience to effectively handle setbacks and maintain motivation.

Key Takeaways:

1. **Reframe Failure:** View failure as valuable feedback that provides insights and learning opportunities rather than as a personal defeat.

2. **Learn and Adapt:** Analyze what went wrong, extract lessons, and adjust your strategies to improve future outcomes.

3. **Develop Resilience:** Build emotional strength and maintain motivation by setting small goals and surrounding yourself with supportive individuals.

By embracing failure and leveraging it as a tool for growth, you can navigate setbacks with confidence, improve your strategies, and move closer to achieving your goals. This shift in perspective transforms failure from a barrier into a powerful catalyst for success.

Chapter 3

The Art of Setting Meaningful Goals

Introduction

Setting goals is a foundational practice for achieving success and fulfilment in life. However, it's not just about setting any goals; it's about setting meaningful, well-defined goals that align with your values and vision. This chapter explores the art of goal setting, emphasizing the importance of clarity, alignment, and actionable steps to ensure that your goals are not only achievable but also deeply motivating.

3.1 The Importance of Meaningful Goals

Definition of Meaningful Goals:

- **Alignment with Values:** Meaningful goals resonate with your core values and long-term vision, giving you a sense of purpose and motivation.
- **Impact on Life:** Goals that align with your values and aspirations contribute significantly to your overall satisfaction and sense of achievement.

Benefits of Setting Meaningful Goals:

- **Increased Motivation:** When goals reflect what truly matters to you, you're more likely to stay motivated and committed.
- **Focused Efforts:** Meaningful goals provide a clear direction and help you focus your efforts on what's most important.
- **Greater Fulfilment:** Achieving goals that align with your values leads to a deeper sense of satisfaction and accomplishment.

3.2 The SMART Framework

Definition of SMART Goals:

- **Specific:** Clearly define what you want to achieve. A specific goal answers the questions: What do I want to accomplish? Why is this goal important? Who is involved? Where is it located? Which resources or limits are involved?
    - *Example:* "I want to increase my sales by 20% over the next quarter."
- **Measurable:** Establish criteria to track your progress and determine when the goal is achieved. This involves quantifying your goal in measurable terms.
    - *Example:* "I will track my sales performance through monthly reports and set milestones at 5% intervals."
- **Achievable:** Ensure that the goal is realistic and attainable given your resources and constraints. Consider if you have the necessary skills, time, and support to achieve it.
    - *Example:* "Given my current sales strategies and resources, a 20% increase is a challenging but achievable target."

- **Relevant:** Align the goal with your broader objectives and values. It should matter to you and contribute to your long-term vision.
    - *Example:* "Increasing sales aligns with my goal of growing my business and advancing my career."
- **Time-bound:** Set a deadline for achieving the goal to create a sense of urgency and prioritize your efforts.
    - *Example:* "I will achieve a 20% increase in sales by the end of the next quarter."

3.3 Aligning Goals with Core Values

Identifying Core Values:

- **Self-Reflection:** Spend time reflecting on what truly matters to you. Consider your passions, beliefs, and what you find most fulfilling.
- **Value Assessment:** Use tools such as values clarification exercises or questionnaires to identify and prioritize your core values.

Aligning Goals with Values:

- **Goal Review:** Evaluate your current goals to ensure they align with your identified values. Make adjustments as needed to reflect what is most important to you.
- **Purpose Connection:** Ensure that each goal contributes to a larger purpose or vision that resonates with your values and long-term aspirations.

3.4 Creating an Action Plan

Breaking Down Goals:

- **Actionable Steps:** Divide larger goals into smaller, actionable tasks. This makes the goal more manageable and provides a clear roadmap for achieving it.
    - *Example:* For increasing sales, actionable steps might include creating a marketing plan, training the sales team, and setting up tracking systems.
- **Timelines and Milestones:** Set specific deadlines and milestones for each task to track progress and stay on schedule.

Monitoring Progress:

- **Regular Check-ins:** Schedule regular check-ins to assess your progress and make necessary adjustments. This helps ensure that you stay on track and adapt to any changes.
- **Adjustments and Flexibility:** Be prepared to adjust your action plan as needed based on your progress and any unforeseen challenges.

3.5 Practical Exercises

Goal Setting Worksheet:

- **Purpose:** To help you define and organize your goals using the SMART framework.
- **Instructions:** Complete the worksheet by defining your goals according to the SMART criteria. Include sections for specifying, measuring, achieving, relevancy, and setting deadlines.

Values Clarification Exercise:

- **Purpose:** To identify and prioritize your core values and align them with your goals.
- **Instructions:** Use the exercise to reflect on and list your core values. Review your goals to ensure they align with these values and make adjustments if needed.

3.6 Summary and Key Takeaways

Summary of Concepts:

- **Meaningful Goals:** Goals should be aligned with your core values and long-term vision to provide motivation and fulfilment.
- **SMART Framework:** Use the SMART criteria to set clear, achievable, and measurable goals with a defined deadline.
- **Action Plan:** Break down goals into actionable steps, set timelines, and regularly monitor progress to stay on track.

Key Takeaways:

1. **Set Meaningful Goals:** Ensure your goals resonate with your core values and contribute to your long-term vision.
2. **Apply SMART Criteria:** Define your goals as Specific, Measurable, Achievable, Relevant, and Time-bound for clarity and focus.
3. **Create an Action Plan:** Develop a detailed action plan with actionable steps, deadlines, and regular progress check-ins to achieve your goals effectively.

By setting and pursuing meaningful goals, you can create a clear path toward achieving your aspirations and living a fulfilling life. The SMART framework and alignment with your core values ensure that your goals are not only attainable but also deeply motivating.

Chapter 4

Building Strong Relationships

Introduction

Strong relationships are the bedrock of personal and professional success. They provide support, enhance collaboration, and contribute significantly to overall well-being and satisfaction. This chapter explores the fundamentals of building and maintaining strong relationships, emphasizing trust, communication, and mutual respect. By understanding and applying these principles, you can cultivate meaningful connections that enrich your life and career.

4.1 The Foundations of Strong Relationships

Trust:

- **Definition and Importance:** Trust is the cornerstone of any strong relationship. It involves reliability, honesty, and integrity. Trust fosters a safe environment where individuals feel valued and understood.

- **Building Trust:** Consistently demonstrate reliability by following through on promises and commitments. Practice honesty and openness, and address issues directly rather than avoiding them.

Communication:

- **Effective Communication:** Clear and effective communication involves not just speaking clearly but also listening actively. It includes verbal and non-verbal communication, such as body language and tone of voice.

- **Active Listening:** Engage in active listening by fully concentrating on the speaker, acknowledging their message, and providing thoughtful responses. Avoid interrupting or making assumptions.

Mutual Respect:

- **Definition and Importance:** Mutual respect means valuing others' opinions, feelings, and needs. It involves recognizing and appreciating the differences in others and treating them with dignity.

- **Practicing Respect:** Show respect by being considerate of others' viewpoints, acknowledging their contributions, and providing constructive feedback rather than criticism.

4.2 Building Personal Relationships

Family and Friends:

- **Nurturing Connections:** Invest time and effort into maintaining relationships with family and friends. Regularly check in, show appreciation, and make time for meaningful interactions.

- **Conflict Resolution:** Address conflicts openly and constructively. Focus on understanding each other's perspectives and finding mutually agreeable solutions.

Romantic Relationships:

- **Communication and Understanding:** Prioritize open communication and empathy in romantic relationships. Discuss expectations, concerns, and aspirations to build a strong foundation.
- **Shared Goals and Values:** Ensure alignment on core values and long-term goals. Shared values foster deeper connections and help navigate challenges together.

4.3 Building Professional Relationships

Networking:

- **Effective Networking:** Build professional relationships by engaging in networking activities, attending industry events, and participating in relevant online communities.
- **Value Exchange:** Focus on creating value for others, not just seeking it. Offer assistance, share insights, and build genuine connections based on mutual interests.

Teamwork and Collaboration:

- **Fostering Team Dynamics:** Create a positive team environment by encouraging collaboration, recognizing contributions, and fostering a sense of camaraderie.
- **Conflict Management:** Address conflicts within teams promptly and constructively. Encourage open dialogue and seek collaborative solutions that benefit the team as a whole.

4.4 Maintaining Strong Relationships

Consistency:

- **Regular Interaction:** Maintain relationships by staying in regular contact and showing consistent support. Consistent interactions build familiarity and reinforce connections.
- **Follow Through:** Follow through on commitments and promises to reinforce trust and reliability.

Adaptability:

- **Embrace Change:** Be adaptable and open to change as relationships evolve over time. Understand that people and circumstances change, and be willing to adjust your approach accordingly.
- **Ongoing Improvement:** Continuously seek ways to improve and strengthen relationships. Regularly evaluate your interactions and seek feedback to enhance your relationship-building skills.

4.5 Practical Exercises

Relationship Reflection Journal:

- **Purpose:** To help you reflect on and assess the quality of your relationships.

- **Instructions:** Use the journal to reflect on key relationships in your life. Assess areas of strength and opportunities for improvement. Set goals for enhancing these relationships and track your progress.

Active Listening Practice:

- **Purpose:** To improve your active listening skills in conversations.
- **Instructions:** Practice active listening by engaging in conversations where you focus solely on listening. Avoid interrupting and summarize what the speaker has said to confirm understanding.

4.6 Summary and Key Takeaways

Summary of Concepts:

- **Trust, Communication, and Respect:** Strong relationships are built on the foundations of trust, effective communication, and mutual respect.
- **Personal and Professional Relationships:** Invest in personal relationships with family and friends, and build professional relationships through networking and teamwork.
- **Consistency and Adaptability:** Maintain relationships through regular interaction and adaptability, continually seeking to improve and strengthen connections.

Key Takeaways:

1. **Build Trust:** Foster trust by being reliable, honest, and open in your interactions.
2. **Communicate Effectively:** Practice clear communication and active listening to enhance understanding and connection.
3. **Show Mutual Respect:** Value others' perspectives and contributions, and address conflicts constructively.
4. **Invest in Relationships:** Nurture personal and professional relationships by staying engaged and adapting to changes.
5. **Reflect and Improve:** Regularly reflect on the quality of your relationships and seek ways to enhance them.

Strong relationships contribute to a fulfilling and successful life. By applying the principles of trust, communication, and respect, and investing in both personal and professional connections, you can build meaningful relationships that support your growth and success.

Chapter 5

Consistency: The Key to Long-Term Success

Introduction

Consistency is often the unsung hero of success. It's the steady, persistent effort that transforms aspirations into achievements. In this chapter, we delve into the importance of consistency, how it impacts your progress toward goals, and practical strategies to cultivate and maintain consistency in your personal and professional life.

5.1 Understanding Consistency

Definition of Consistency:

- **Steady Action:** Consistency involves performing actions in a reliable and repeatable manner over time. It means adhering to routines and practices that align with your goals and values.

- **Long-Term Commitment:** It's about maintaining a commitment to your objectives, regardless of obstacles or fluctuations in motivation.

Importance of Consistency:

- **Builds Habits:** Consistent actions help establish positive habits, making it easier to achieve long-term goals.

- **Enhances Skill Development:** Repeated practice leads to skill improvement and mastery. Consistency accelerates the learning curve and builds expertise.

- **Creates Momentum:** Regular efforts build momentum, making it easier to maintain progress and achieve milestones.

5.2 The Role of Habits in Consistency

Forming Positive Habits:

- **Start Small:** Begin with small, manageable actions that you can easily integrate into your routine. Gradually increase the complexity as the habit becomes established.

- **Consistency Over Perfection:** Focus on consistent practice rather than perfection. It's more important to perform a task regularly than to execute it flawlessly.

Maintaining Habits:

- **Use Triggers:** Link new habits to existing routines or triggers. For example, if you want to establish a habit of exercising, do it immediately after your morning coffee.

- **Track Progress:** Use habit-tracking tools or journals to monitor your progress. This helps reinforce commitment and provides a visual representation of your consistency.

5.3 Overcoming Challenges to Consistency

Identifying Obstacles:

- **Lack of Motivation:** Motivation can fluctuate, making it challenging to maintain consistency. Develop strategies to stay motivated, such as setting clear goals and visualizing success.
- **Time Constraints:** Busy schedules can disrupt consistency. Prioritize tasks and create a schedule that allocates time for essential activities.

Strategies for Overcoming Challenges:

- **Create a Routine:** Establish a daily or weekly routine that includes time for your key activities. Routines help make actions habitual and less dependent on fluctuating motivation.
- **Seek Accountability:** Share your goals with a friend, mentor, or coach who can provide encouragement and hold you accountable for your commitments.

5.4 Leveraging Consistency for Long-Term Success

Achieving Goals:

- **Break Down Goals:** Divide larger goals into smaller, actionable steps. Consistent progress on these smaller steps leads to the achievement of the larger goal.
- **Celebrate Milestones:** Recognize and celebrate milestones along the way to maintain motivation and reinforce your commitment.

Building Reputation:

- **Professional Credibility:** Consistency in your work and interactions builds trust and credibility with colleagues, clients, and partners.
- **Personal Integrity:** Being consistent in your values and actions enhances your personal integrity and strengthens relationships.

5.5 Practical Exercises

Consistency Planning Worksheet:

- **Purpose:** To help you plan and maintain consistency in your actions.
- **Instructions:** Use the worksheet to outline your goals, identify key actions needed to achieve them, and create a schedule for regular tasks. Include sections for tracking progress and adjusting plans as needed.

Habit Formation Tracker:

- **Purpose:** To assist in developing and maintaining new habits.
- **Instructions:** Create a tracker with a calendar or checklist format. Mark off each day you successfully perform the new habit. Review your progress regularly and adjust your approach as needed.

5.6 Summary and Key Takeaways

Summary of Concepts:

- **Importance of Consistency:** Consistency is crucial for forming habits, developing skills, and building momentum toward long-term success.

- **Overcoming Challenges:** Address obstacles such as fluctuating motivation and time constraints by creating routines, using triggers, and seeking accountability.

- **Leveraging Consistency:** Consistent efforts lead to goal achievement and build professional credibility and personal integrity.

Key Takeaways:

1. **Build Habits Gradually:** Start with small, manageable actions to form positive habits, and focus on consistent practice rather than perfection.

2. **Address Challenges:** Identify and address obstacles to consistency by creating routines, managing time effectively, and seeking accountability.

3. **Celebrate Progress:** Recognize and celebrate milestones to maintain motivation and reinforce your commitment to your goals.

Consistency is the key that unlocks long-term success. By cultivating consistent habits, overcoming challenges, and leveraging your efforts toward achieving your goals, you can create lasting progress and fulfilment in both your personal and professional life.

Chapter 6

The Art of Time Management

Introduction

Time management is a critical skill that influences every aspect of our lives. Mastering the art of time management enables you to balance multiple responsibilities, achieve your goals efficiently, and reduce stress. This chapter explores effective strategies for managing your time, prioritizing tasks, and creating a productive environment to maximize your efficiency and success.

6.1 The Principles of Effective Time Management

Understanding Time Management:

- **Definition:** Time management involves planning and controlling how much time to spend on specific activities. Effective time management helps you work smarter, not harder, to accomplish your goals.

- **Benefits:** Proper time management leads to increased productivity, reduced stress, and better work-life balance. It allows you to accomplish more in less time and prioritize what truly matters.

Core Principles:

- **Prioritization:** Focus on what's most important and urgent. Use methods such as the Eisenhower Matrix or Pareto Principle (80/20 Rule) to prioritize tasks.

- **Goal Setting:** Set clear, achievable goals to guide your time management efforts. Align your daily activities with your long-term objectives.

- **Planning:** Develop a structured plan for your tasks and activities. Use tools such as planners, calendars, and to-do lists to organize and track your responsibilities.

6.2 Prioritizing Tasks

The Eisenhower Matrix:

- **Urgent vs. Important:** The Eisenhower Matrix helps categorize tasks into four quadrants:
    1. **Urgent and Important:** Tasks that require immediate attention (e.g., deadlines).
    2. **Important but Not Urgent:** Tasks that contribute to long-term goals (e.g., strategic planning).
    3. **Urgent but Not Important:** Tasks that are pressing but not critical (e.g., interruptions).
    4. **Not Urgent and Not Important:** Tasks that offer little value (e.g., excessive social media).

The Pareto Principle (80/20 Rule):

- **Focus on Impact:** Identify the 20% of tasks that contribute to 80% of your results. Concentrate your efforts on these high-impact activities to maximize efficiency and outcomes.

6.3 Creating and Managing Schedules

Daily and Weekly Planning:

- **Daily Schedule:** Plan your day by allocating specific time blocks for tasks and activities. Include breaks to maintain productivity and avoid burnout.
- **Weekly Overview:** Develop a weekly schedule to manage longer-term projects and commitments. Review and adjust your plan based on priorities and deadlines.

Time Blocking:

- **Definition:** Time blocking involves scheduling specific blocks of time for focused work on individual tasks or projects.
- **Benefits:** This technique helps prevent multitasking, reduces distractions, and ensures dedicated time for each activity. It enhances focus and productivity.

6.4 Overcoming Procrastination

Identifying Causes:

- **Common Reasons:** Procrastination can stem from various factors, including fear of failure, perfectionism, or lack of motivation.
- **Self-Assessment:** Reflect on your reasons for procrastination and identify patterns or triggers that contribute to delays.

Strategies to Overcome Procrastination:

- **Break Tasks into Smaller Steps:** Divide large tasks into smaller, manageable parts. This makes the task less daunting and easier to start.
- **Set Deadlines and Use Timers:** Establish deadlines for tasks and use timers to create a sense of urgency. The Pomodoro Technique, which involves working for 25 minutes followed by a 5-minute break, is effective for maintaining focus.

6.5 Creating a Productive Environment

Organize Your Workspace:

- **Declutter:** Keep your workspace organized and free of distractions. An orderly environment promotes focus and efficiency.
- **Ergonomics:** Ensure that your workspace is ergonomically designed to prevent discomfort and enhance productivity.

Minimize Distractions:

- **Identify Distractions:** Recognize common distractions in your environment, such as social media or noisy surroundings.

- **Implement Solutions:** Use strategies such as turning off notifications, setting boundaries for interruptions, and creating a quiet work area.

6.6 Practical Exercises

Time Management Planner:

- **Purpose:** To help you plan and manage your time effectively.
- **Instructions:** Use the planner to schedule daily and weekly tasks, set priorities, and allocate time blocks for focused work. Include sections for tracking progress and reflecting on time management practices.

Procrastination Journal:

- **Purpose:** To identify and address procrastination patterns.
- **Instructions:** Maintain a journal to record instances of procrastination, identify triggers, and document strategies used to overcome delays. Reflect on your progress and adjust your approach as needed.

6.7 Summary and Key Takeaways

Summary of Concepts:

- **Principles of Time Management:** Effective time management involves prioritization, goal setting, and planning to maximize productivity and reduce stress.
- **Prioritization Techniques:** Use methods such as the Eisenhower Matrix and Pareto Principle to focus on high-impact tasks.
- **Scheduling and Procrastination:** Create structured schedules, use time blocking, and address procrastination with practical strategies.

Key Takeaways:

1. **Prioritize Effectively:** Use prioritization techniques to focus on tasks that contribute most to your goals and results.
2. **Plan and Schedule:** Develop daily and weekly plans, use time blocking, and manage your schedule to enhance productivity.
3. **Overcome Procrastination:** Break tasks into smaller steps, set deadlines, and use timers to overcome procrastination and maintain focus.
4. **Create a Productive Environment:** Organize your workspace, minimize distractions, and implement ergonomic solutions to boost efficiency.

Mastering time management enables you to achieve your goals efficiently, reduce stress, and maintain a balanced life. By applying effective strategies and techniques, you can transform how you manage your time, leading to greater success and fulfilment in all areas of your life.

Chapter 7

The Power of Positive Thinking

Introduction

Positive thinking is more than just a feel-good concept; it's a powerful approach that can significantly impact your overall well-being and success. This chapter delves into the science and practice of positive thinking, exploring how maintaining an optimistic mindset can lead to improved mental health, better decision-making, and enhanced performance in various aspects of life.

7.1 Understanding Positive Thinking

Definition and Concept:

- **Positive Thinking:** Positive thinking involves focusing on the good aspects of any situation and expecting favorable outcomes. It's about cultivating an optimistic attitude and seeing opportunities rather than obstacles.

- **Impact on Life:** Adopting a positive mindset can improve resilience, enhance relationships, and contribute to achieving personal and professional goals.

Scientific Basis:

- **Research Findings:** Studies have shown that positive thinking is associated with better health outcomes, increased longevity, and improved quality of life. Positive thinkers are more likely to engage in healthy behaviors and experience lower levels of stress.

- **Neuroscience Insights:** Positive thinking can influence brain function, including areas related to stress regulation, emotion processing, and decision-making.

7.2 Benefits of Positive Thinking

Mental Health:

- **Stress Reduction:** Positive thinking helps mitigate the effects of stress by fostering a more balanced perspective. It can reduce anxiety and promote emotional stability.

- **Enhanced Resilience:** An optimistic mindset improves resilience, enabling individuals to cope with adversity more effectively and recover from setbacks.

Physical Health:

- **Improved Immune Function:** Positive emotions are linked to a stronger immune system, reducing susceptibility to illness and promoting overall health.

- **Increased Energy:** A positive outlook can boost energy levels and motivation, leading to greater engagement in physical activities and better health outcomes.

Personal and Professional Success:

- **Goal Achievement:** Positive thinking enhances motivation and persistence, leading to greater effort and focus on achieving goals.

- **Improved Relationships:** An optimistic attitude fosters better interpersonal relationships, enhancing communication, empathy, and collaboration.

7.3 Cultivating a Positive Mindset

Techniques for Positive Thinking:

- **Gratitude Practice:** Regularly acknowledging and appreciating the positive aspects of your life can shift focus away from negativity. Keep a gratitude journal to record and reflect on things you are thankful for.
- **Affirmations:** Use positive affirmations to reinforce optimistic beliefs and counteract negative self-talk. Repeat affirmations daily to build confidence and self-worth.
- **Visualization:** Practice visualizing positive outcomes and successes. This technique helps create a mental image of achieving your goals, enhancing motivation and focus.

Reframing Negative Thoughts:

- **Cognitive Restructuring:** Challenge and reframe negative thoughts by identifying irrational beliefs and replacing them with more balanced, positive perspectives.
- **Perspective Shifting:** Focus on the potential benefits and opportunities in challenging situations. Reframe setbacks as learning experiences and growth opportunities.

7.4 Managing Negative Influences

Identifying Negative Influences:

- **Internal Factors:** Recognize internal negative thought patterns and self-doubt. Self-awareness is key to addressing and transforming these negative beliefs.
- **External Factors:** Identify external sources of negativity, such as unsupportive people or toxic environments. Minimize exposure to these influences where possible.

Strategies for Addressing Negativity:

- **Positive Social Networks:** Surround yourself with supportive and optimistic individuals who uplift and encourage you. Build relationships with people who share your positive outlook.
- **Healthy Boundaries:** Set boundaries to protect yourself from negative influences and prioritize activities and environments that foster positivity.

7.5 Practical Exercises

Gratitude Journal Exercise:

- **Purpose:** To cultivate a habit of recognizing and appreciating positive aspects of your life.
- **Instructions:** Dedicate time each day to write down three things you are grateful for. Reflect on these entries regularly to reinforce a positive mindset.

Affirmations Practice:

- **Purpose:** To build self-confidence and counteract negative self-talk.

- **Instructions:** Create a list of positive affirmations related to your goals and values. Repeat these affirmations daily, ideally in front of a mirror, to internalize positive beliefs.

Visualization Exercise:

- **Purpose:** To enhance motivation and focus on achieving goals.
- **Instructions:** Spend a few minutes each day visualizing yourself achieving your goals. Create a detailed mental image of the process and the successful outcome, engaging all your senses.

7.6 Summary and Key Takeaways

Summary of Concepts:

- **Positive Thinking:** An optimistic mindset improves mental and physical health, enhances personal and professional success, and fosters resilience.
- **Cultivating Positivity:** Use techniques such as gratitude practice, affirmations, and visualization to build and maintain a positive outlook.
- **Managing Negativity:** Identify and address negative influences by surrounding yourself with supportive individuals and setting healthy boundaries.

Key Takeaways:

1. **Embrace Positivity:** Cultivate a positive mindset to enhance resilience, improve health, and achieve success.
2. **Practice Gratitude and Affirmations:** Regularly practice gratitude and use affirmations to reinforce positive beliefs and boost confidence.
3. **Visualize Success:** Engage in visualization exercises to create a mental image of achieving your goals and enhance motivation.
4. **Address Negativity:** Manage negative influences by building positive social networks and setting boundaries.

Chapter 8

Mastering Financial Management

Introduction

Financial management is a crucial skill that impacts every facet of your life, from achieving your personal goals to ensuring long-term security and stability. This chapter explores essential principles and strategies for mastering financial management, including budgeting, saving, investing, and managing debt. By understanding and applying these concepts, you can take control of your financial future and build a strong foundation for success.

8.1 Understanding Financial Management

Definition and Importance:

- **Financial Management:** Financial management involves planning, organizing, controlling, and monitoring financial resources to achieve personal and professional objectives.
- **Benefits:** Effective financial management helps you achieve financial goals, avoid unnecessary debt, and build wealth. It provides a clear roadmap for managing your money and making informed decisions.

Core Components:

- **Budgeting:** The process of creating a plan for your income and expenses to ensure you live within your means and save for future goals.
- **Saving:** Setting aside a portion of your income for future needs or emergencies. Saving helps you build an emergency fund and achieve financial goals.
- **Investing:** Allocating money to assets or ventures with the expectation of generating returns. Investing helps grow your wealth over time.
- **Debt Management:** Strategies for managing and reducing debt to maintain financial health and avoid financial strain.

8.2 Creating a Budget

The Budgeting Process:

- **Track Your Income and Expenses:** Start by tracking all sources of income and expenses to understand your current financial situation. Use tools such as spreadsheets or budgeting apps to record and categorize transactions.
- **Set Financial Goals:** Establish short-term and long-term financial goals, such as saving for a vacation, paying off debt, or building an emergency fund. Align your budget with these goals.
- **Allocate Funds:** Create a budget that allocates funds to essential expenses (e.g., housing, utilities, groceries), savings, and discretionary spending. Ensure that your spending aligns with your financial goals.

Budgeting Techniques:

- **The 50/30/20 Rule:** Allocate 50% of your income to needs, 30% to wants, and 20% to savings and debt repayment. This simple rule provides a balanced approach to budgeting.
- **Zero-Based Budgeting:** Allocate every dollar of your income to specific expenses, savings, or debt repayment, ensuring that your budget balances to zero at the end of each month.

8.3 Building and Maintaining Savings

Creating an Emergency Fund:

- **Purpose:** An emergency fund provides a financial cushion for unexpected expenses, such as medical emergencies or car repairs.
- **How to Build:** Aim to save three to six months' worth of living expenses in a separate savings account. Contribute regularly to build and maintain your emergency fund.

Saving for Goals:

- **Short-Term Goals:** Set aside money for short-term goals, such as vacations or major purchases. Use high-yield savings accounts or certificates of deposit (CDs) for better returns.
- **Long-Term Goals:** Save for long-term goals, such as retirement or purchasing a home, by investing in retirement accounts (e.g., 401(k), IRA) or other investment vehicles.

8.4 Investing for the Future

Investment Basics:

- **Types of Investments:** Understand different investment options, including stocks, bonds, mutual funds, and real estate. Each type has its own risk and return profile.
- **Diversification:** Spread your investments across various asset classes to reduce risk and increase the potential for returns. Diversification helps protect your portfolio from market fluctuations.

Investment Strategies:

- **Long-Term Investing:** Focus on long-term growth by investing in assets with the potential for high returns over time. Avoid making impulsive decisions based on short-term market movements.
- **Dollar-Cost Averaging:** Invest a fixed amount of money at regular intervals, regardless of market conditions. This strategy helps reduce the impact of market volatility and lowers the average cost of investments.

8.5 Managing and Reducing Debt

Types of Debt:

- **Good Debt vs. Bad Debt:** Good debt, such as a mortgage or student loans, is used for investments that can build wealth or improve your future earning potential. Bad debt, such as high-interest credit card debt, can hinder financial progress.

- **Debt Management Strategies:** Focus on paying off high-interest debt first, using methods such as the debt snowball or avalanche approach. Consolidate or refinance debt if it helps reduce interest rates and monthly payments.

Preventing Future Debt:

- **Create a Debt Repayment Plan:** Develop a plan to manage and pay off existing debt. Prioritize consistent payments and avoid accumulating new debt.

- **Build an Emergency Fund:** An emergency fund helps prevent reliance on credit cards or loans during unexpected financial challenges.

8.6 Practical Exercises

Budgeting Worksheet:

- **Purpose:** To help you create and maintain a budget that aligns with your financial goals.

- **Instructions:** Use the worksheet to track your income and expenses, set financial goals, and allocate funds accordingly. Review and adjust your budget regularly based on your financial situation.

Savings Tracker:

- **Purpose:** To monitor and manage your savings for short-term and long-term goals.

- **Instructions:** Use the tracker to set savings goals, record contributions, and monitor progress. Adjust your savings plan as needed to stay on track.

Debt Repayment Plan:

- **Purpose:** To develop a strategy for managing and reducing debt.

- **Instructions:** List all your debts, including amounts, interest rates, and minimum payments. Choose a repayment method, such as the snowball or avalanche approach, and create a plan to pay off debt systematically.

8.7 Summary and Key Takeaways

Summary of Concepts:

- **Financial Management:** Effective financial management involves budgeting, saving, investing, and managing debt to achieve personal and professional goals.

- **Budgeting:** Create a budget by tracking income and expenses, setting financial goals, and allocating funds. Use techniques such as the 50/30/20 rule or zero-based budgeting.

- **Savings and Investing:** Build an emergency fund, save for short-term and long-term goals, and invest in diversified assets to grow your wealth.

- **Debt Management:** Understand different types of debt, prioritize debt repayment, and develop strategies to manage and reduce debt.

Key Takeaways:

1. **Create a Budget:** Track your income and expenses, set financial goals, and allocate funds to manage your finances effectively.

2. **Build Savings:** Establish an emergency fund and save for both short-term and long-term goals to secure your financial future.

3. **Invest Wisely:** Understand different investment options, diversify your portfolio, and focus on long-term growth.

4. **Manage Debt:** Prioritize paying off high-interest debt, create a debt repayment plan, and prevent future debt by maintaining financial discipline.

Mastering financial management is essential for achieving financial stability, reaching your goals, and ensuring long-term success. By applying these principles and strategies, you can take control of your finances, build wealth, and enjoy greater peace of mind.

Chapter 9
Embracing Lifelong Learning

Introduction

Lifelong learning is a fundamental concept that drives personal and professional growth. In a rapidly changing world, the ability to continuously acquire new knowledge and skills is essential for adapting to new challenges, seizing opportunities, and achieving long-term success. This chapter explores the importance of lifelong learning, strategies for cultivating a learning mindset, and practical approaches to integrate learning into your daily life.

9.1 The Importance of Lifelong Learning

Definition and Concept:

- **Lifelong Learning:** Lifelong learning involves continually acquiring knowledge or skills throughout your life, beyond formal education. It encompasses personal growth, professional development, and adapting to new challenges.
- **Benefits:** Lifelong learning enhances your adaptability, keeps you competitive in your field, and enriches your personal life. It fosters intellectual curiosity, helps you stay updated with advancements, and promotes personal fulfilment.

Impact on Personal and Professional Growth:

- **Career Advancement:** Continuous learning helps you stay relevant in your career, improve job performance, and open doors to new opportunities. It demonstrates commitment to personal growth and adaptability.
- **Personal Development:** Lifelong learning fosters personal growth by expanding your horizons, enhancing critical thinking, and encouraging self-discovery. It enriches your life experiences and broadens your understanding of the world.

9.2 Cultivating a Learning Mindset

Adopting a Growth Mindset:

- **Definition:** A growth mindset is the belief that abilities and intelligence can be developed through effort and learning. It contrasts with a fixed mindset, which views abilities as static and unchangeable.
- **Benefits:** Embracing a growth mindset encourages resilience, curiosity, and a willingness to embrace challenges. It fosters a positive attitude toward learning and improvement.

Overcoming Learning Barriers:

- **Fear of Failure:** Overcome the fear of failure by viewing mistakes as learning opportunities rather than setbacks. Embrace challenges and persist in the face of difficulties.

- **Lack of Time:** Incorporate learning into your daily routine by setting aside dedicated time for reading, courses, or skill development. Leverage small pockets of time, such as during commutes or breaks, for learning activities.

9.3 Strategies for Lifelong Learning

Setting Learning Goals:

- **Identify Interests and Needs:** Determine areas of interest or skills you want to develop. Set specific, measurable, achievable, relevant, and time-bound (SMART) goals to guide your learning journey.
- **Create a Learning Plan:** Develop a plan outlining the steps and resources needed to achieve your learning goals. Include milestones and deadlines to track your progress.

Exploring Learning Resources:

- **Formal Education:** Consider enrolling in courses, workshops, or degree programs offered by educational institutions. Online platforms like Coursera, Udemy, and Khan Academy offer a wide range of courses on various topics.
- **Self-Directed Learning:** Utilize books, articles, podcasts, and videos to explore new subjects. Join discussion groups or online forums to engage with others interested in similar topics.
- **Networking:** Connect with mentors, colleagues, or industry experts to gain insights and advice. Attend conferences, seminars, or webinars to stay informed about advancements in your field.

9.4 Integrating Learning into Daily Life

Developing Learning Habits:

- **Daily Reading:** Incorporate reading into your daily routine, whether through books, articles, or industry publications. Aim for a specific amount of reading time each day to stay informed and inspired.
- **Skill Practice:** Allocate time for practicing new skills or applying knowledge in real-life scenarios. Engage in projects or hobbies that challenge and develop your abilities.

Embracing Technology:

- **Learning Apps:** Use learning apps and platforms to access educational content, track progress, and stay motivated. Many apps offer interactive and engaging ways to learn new skills.
- **Online Communities:** Participate in online communities or forums related to your interests. Engage in discussions, share knowledge, and learn from others' experiences.

9.5 Practical Exercises

Learning Goal Worksheet:

- **Purpose:** To help you set and track learning goals effectively.

- **Instructions:** Use the worksheet to identify areas of interest, set SMART learning goals, and develop a plan for achieving them. Include sections for tracking progress and adjusting your plan as needed.

Daily Learning Log:

- **Purpose:** To monitor and reflect on your daily learning activities.
- **Instructions:** Maintain a log to record what you've learned each day, including new skills, insights, or resources explored. Reflect on your progress and set new learning objectives.

Skill Practice Plan:

- **Purpose:** To integrate skill practice into your routine.
- **Instructions:** Develop a plan outlining specific skills to practice, the frequency of practice, and ways to apply the skills in real-life situations. Track your progress and adjust your plan based on your learning experiences.

9.6 Summary and Key Takeaways

Summary of Concepts:

- **Lifelong Learning:** Lifelong learning involves continuously acquiring knowledge and skills to enhance personal and professional growth. It fosters adaptability, intellectual curiosity, and personal fulfilment.
- **Cultivating a Learning Mindset:** Embrace a growth mindset, overcome barriers to learning, and integrate learning into your daily life.
- **Strategies and Resources:** Set learning goals, explore various resources, and use technology to support your learning journey.

Key Takeaways:

1. **Embrace Lifelong Learning:** Continuously seek opportunities to acquire new knowledge and skills to stay relevant and fulfilled.
2. **Adopt a Growth Mindset:** Cultivate a mindset that views challenges as opportunities for growth and learning.
3. **Set Learning Goals:** Identify areas of interest, set SMART goals, and create a plan to guide your learning journey.

Lifelong learning is the key to staying adaptable, achieving personal and professional success, and leading a fulfilling life. By committing to ongoing education and growth, you can navigate an ever-changing world with confidence and resilience.

Chapter 10

Building Resilience and Overcoming Adversity

Introduction

Resilience is the ability to bounce back from setbacks, adapt to change, and continue pursuing your goals despite difficulties. It's a crucial skill that enables you to navigate life's challenges effectively and maintain mental and emotional well-being. This chapter explores the concept of resilience, strategies for developing it, and practical approaches for overcoming adversity and thriving in the face of challenges.

10.1 Understanding Resilience

Definition and Importance:

- **Resilience:** Resilience is the capacity to recover quickly from difficulties, adapt to challenging circumstances, and maintain a positive outlook despite adversity.

- **Benefits:** Building resilience enhances your ability to cope with stress, recover from setbacks, and achieve long-term success. It promotes mental strength, emotional stability, and overall well-being.

Core Components of Resilience:

- **Emotional Regulation:** The ability to manage and express emotions constructively, even in stressful situations.

- **Optimism:** Maintaining a positive outlook and focusing on potential solutions rather than dwelling on problems.

- **Adaptability:** The capacity to adjust to new circumstances and embrace change with flexibility.

10.2 Developing Resilience

Building Emotional Strength:

- **Self-Awareness:** Develop self-awareness to understand your emotional responses and triggers. Reflect on your experiences and identify patterns in how you handle stress and adversity.

- **Emotional Regulation Techniques:** Practice techniques such as mindfulness, deep breathing, and progressive muscle relaxation to manage stress and maintain emotional balance.

Cultivating Optimism:

- **Positive Reframing:** Reframe negative situations by focusing on potential benefits and opportunities. Challenge negative thoughts and replace them with more balanced perspectives.

- **Gratitude Practice:** Regularly practice gratitude to shift your focus toward positive aspects of your life. Acknowledge and appreciate the good things, even during challenging times.

Enhancing Adaptability:

- **Embrace Change:** View change as an opportunity for growth rather than a threat. Develop a flexible mindset that allows you to adapt to new circumstances with ease.
- **Develop Problem-Solving Skills:** Strengthen your problem-solving abilities by approaching challenges with creativity and resourcefulness. Break problems into manageable parts and explore multiple solutions.

10.3 Strategies for Overcoming Adversity

Problem-Solving Approaches:

- **Identify the Problem:** Clearly define the problem or challenge you are facing. Gather relevant information and understand the root causes of the issue.
- **Develop an Action Plan:** Create a plan outlining specific steps to address the problem. Set realistic goals and prioritize actions based on their impact and feasibility.
- **Seek Support:** Reach out to mentors, friends, or support networks for guidance and assistance. Collaborate with others to gain different perspectives and solutions.

Building a Support Network:

- **Social Connections:** Cultivate strong relationships with supportive individuals who can offer encouragement and assistance during difficult times. Build a network of friends, family, and colleagues who can provide emotional support.
- **Professional Help:** Seek professional support, such as counseling or therapy, if needed. Mental health professionals can provide guidance and coping strategies for managing adversity.

Maintaining Perspective:

- **Focus on Long-Term Goals:** Keep your long-term goals and values in mind when facing challenges. Maintain perspective on the broader picture and remember why you started pursuing your goals.
- **Celebrate Progress:** Acknowledge and celebrate your progress, no matter how small. Recognize your achievements and milestones to stay motivated and focused.

10.4 Practical Exercises

Resilience Journal:

- **Purpose:** To enhance self-awareness and track your resilience-building efforts.
- **Instructions:** Maintain a journal to record your experiences with adversity, your emotional responses, and the strategies you used to overcome challenges. Reflect on your progress and identify areas for improvement.

Positive Reframing Exercise:

- **Purpose:** To practice reframing negative situations and fostering optimism.
- **Instructions:** Identify a recent challenging situation and write down your initial negative thoughts. Then, reframe these thoughts by exploring potential positive outcomes and alternative perspectives.

Adaptability Practice Plan:

- **Purpose:** To develop and strengthen adaptability skills.
- **Instructions:** Create a plan to expose yourself to new experiences or changes. Set specific goals for trying new activities, learning new skills, or adapting to new environments. Reflect on your experiences and adjust your plan as needed.

10.5 Summary and Key Takeaways

Summary of Concepts:

- **Resilience:** Resilience is the ability to recover from setbacks, adapt to change, and maintain a positive outlook. It involves emotional regulation, optimism, and adaptability.
- **Developing Resilience:** Build emotional strength through self-awareness and regulation techniques. Cultivate optimism through positive reframing and gratitude practice. Enhance adaptability by embracing change and developing problem-solving skills.
- **Overcoming Adversity:** Use problem-solving approaches, build a supportive network, and maintain perspective to navigate challenges effectively.

Key Takeaways:

1. **Build Emotional Strength:** Develop self-awareness and practice emotional regulation techniques to manage stress and maintain balance.
2. **Cultivate Optimism:** Reframe negative situations, practice gratitude, and focus on positive aspects of your life to foster resilience.
3. **Enhance Adaptability:** Embrace change, develop problem-solving skills, and approach challenges with flexibility and creativity.
4. **Seek Support:** Build a strong support network and seek professional help if needed to overcome adversity and achieve your goals.

Resilience is a vital skill that empowers you to navigate life's challenges and continue pursuing your goals with determination and strength. By developing resilience and applying practical strategies for overcoming adversity, you can thrive in the face of difficulties and achieve long-term success.

Summary

"Unlocking Life's Secrets: Timeless Wisdom for Achieving True Success" is a comprehensive guide to understanding and applying fundamental principles that lead to a balanced, fulfilling, and successful life. Each chapter provides deep insights into essential aspects of personal and professional development, drawing from ancient wisdom and modern practices.

5. **Mindset:** The book starts by exploring the power of mindset, emphasizing the importance of cultivating a growth mindset. A growth mindset allows individuals to embrace challenges, learn from failures, and persist through difficulties, paving the way for personal and professional success.

6. **Failure:** It reframes failure as a stepping stone rather than a setback. By learning from failures and developing resilience, readers can turn challenges into opportunities for growth and innovation.

7. **Goal Setting:** The book outlines the art of setting meaningful goals. It provides a framework for creating SMART goals and ensuring they align with one's core values, thereby setting a clear path toward achieving long-term aspirations.

8. **Relationships:** Strong, supportive relationships are crucial for success. The book explores strategies for building and maintaining meaningful personal and professional relationships, focusing on trust, communication, and mutual support.

9. **Consistency:** Consistency is highlighted as a key to achieving long-term success. It provides practical advice on developing and maintaining habits, overcoming obstacles, and staying motivated to achieve goals.

10. **Self-Care:** The importance of self-care is emphasized, advocating for a balanced approach to achieving success without compromising personal well-being. It includes strategies for physical, emotional, and social self-care.

11. **Adaptability:** In a constantly changing world, adaptability is essential. The book discusses how to embrace change, develop adaptability skills, and turn challenges into opportunities for growth.

12. **Emotional Intelligence:** The role of emotional intelligence (EI) in personal and professional success is examined. It provides tools for developing self-awareness, empathy, and effective communication skills.

13. **Persistence:** Persistence is identified as a crucial trait for overcoming obstacles and achieving success. The book offers techniques for cultivating perseverance and maintaining motivation through challenges.

14. **Purpose:** Finally, the book guides readers in discovering and living with purpose. It explores how aligning actions with one's core values and purpose leads to a more fulfilling and meaningful life.

Key Takeaways

1. **Adopt a Growth Mindset:** Cultivate a mindset that embraces challenges and views failures as opportunities for growth.

2. **Learn from Failure:** Reframe failure as a valuable learning experience and develop resilience to bounce back stronger.

3. **Set Meaningful Goals:** Create SMART goals that align with your core values and long-term vision for success.

4. **Build Strong Relationships:** Focus on trust, effective communication, and mutual support to nurture personal and professional relationships.

5. **Embrace Consistency:** Develop and maintain consistent habits and routines to achieve long-term success.

6. **Prioritize Self-Care:** Balance your ambitions with self-care practices to maintain overall well-being.

7. **Develop Adaptability:** Stay flexible and turn change into an advantage by developing adaptability skills.

8. **Enhance Emotional Intelligence:** Improve self-awareness, empathy, and communication to strengthen personal and professional relationships.

9. **Cultivate Persistence:** Use persistence and motivation to overcome obstacles and achieve your goals.

10. **Live with Purpose:** Align your actions with your core values and purpose to lead a fulfilling and meaningful life.

The book provides a holistic approach to success, integrating practical advice with timeless wisdom. By applying these principles, readers can unlock their potential, navigate challenges, and achieve a balanced and successful life.

Epilogue

A Journey of Continuous Growth

Introduction

As we reach the end of this exploration into the principles of success and personal development, it's essential to reflect on the journey we've undertaken. The path to success is not a linear one but a continuous journey of growth, learning, and transformation. This epilogue serves as a reminder of the key themes discussed throughout the book and offers guidance on how to carry these lessons forward into your life.

Reflecting on the Journey

Embracing the Process:

- **Growth is Ongoing:** Success and personal development are not final destinations but ongoing processes. Embrace the journey as a series of evolving stages where each experience contributes to your growth and understanding.

- **Learning from Experience:** Every challenge and achievement offers valuable lessons. Reflect on your experiences, learn from them, and use them as stepping stones to further personal and professional development.

The Role of Self-Discovery:

- **Know Yourself:** Understanding your strengths, weaknesses, values, and passions is crucial. Self-discovery helps you align your goals with your true self and makes your journey more meaningful and fulfilling.

- **Adapt and Evolve:** As you grow and change, so will your goals and aspirations. Be open to adjusting your path based on new insights and experiences. Embrace change as a natural part of growth.

Carrying Forward the Lessons

Integrating Key Principles:

- **Vision and Goals:** Continue to set and pursue clear, actionable goals. Your vision should guide your decisions and actions, keeping you focused on what truly matters to you.

- **Positive Mindset:** Maintain a positive outlook and practice resilience. Use the principles of positive thinking to navigate challenges and stay motivated.

- **Financial Management:** Apply the financial strategies discussed to manage your resources wisely, ensuring long-term stability and success.

- **Lifelong Learning:** Commit to ongoing education and self-improvement. Seek new knowledge and skills, and embrace the opportunities for growth that come your way.

- **Resilience:** Develop and reinforce your resilience. Use the strategies learned to overcome adversity and continue progressing toward your goals.

The Importance of Community and Support

Building Relationships:

- **Connect with Others:** Surround yourself with supportive and like-minded individuals. Building a strong network of friends, mentors, and colleagues can provide encouragement, advice, and opportunities.//
- **Give Back:** Share your knowledge and experiences with others. Mentoring and supporting others can reinforce your own learning and contribute to the success of your community.

Celebrating Achievements:

- **Acknowledge Milestones:** Recognize and celebrate your achievements, no matter how small. Celebrating progress helps maintain motivation and reinforces your commitment to your goals.
- **Reflect and Appreciate:** Take time to appreciate how far you've come and the growth you've achieved. Reflection fosters gratitude and provides motivation for future endeavors.

Looking Ahead

Setting New Goals:

- **Evolve Your Vision:** As you achieve your goals, set new ones that challenge and inspire you. Continuously evolving your vision ensures that you remain engaged and motivated in your journey.
- **Pursue New Opportunities:** Be open to exploring new interests and opportunities. Life is full of possibilities, and embracing new challenges can lead to unexpected growth and success.

Maintaining Balance:

- **Prioritize Well-Being:** Ensure that your pursuit of success is balanced with attention to your physical, emotional, and mental well-being. Strive for harmony between personal and professional life.
- **Practice Gratitude:** Maintain a sense of gratitude for your experiences and the people who support you. Gratitude enhances happiness and fosters a positive outlook on life.

Conclusion

The journey of success and personal growth is a dynamic and ongoing process. By integrating the lessons and principles discussed in this book into your daily life, you can continue to evolve, achieve your goals, and lead a fulfilling and meaningful life. Remember, the pursuit of success is not just about reaching a destination but about growing, learning, and thriving every step of the way.

As you move forward, embrace the journey with an open heart and mind. Celebrate your progress, stay curious, and remain resilientContinue to grow, adapt, and pursue your dreams with passion and purpose. The journey of continuous growth is both a privilege and a responsibility—one that offers endless opportunities for discovery, achievement, and joy.

Appendices

Appendix A: Resources and Tools

This appendix provides a curated list of resources and tools to support your journey of personal development and success. These resources will help you delve deeper into the topics discussed in the book and provide additional support as you implement the strategies and principles outlined.

Books

1. **"Atomic Habits: An Easy & Proven Way to Build Good Habits & Break Bad Ones" by James Clear**
    - Explores strategies for habit formation and personal growth through small, incremental changes.

2. **"Mindset: The New Psychology of Success" by Carol S. Dweck**
    - Offers insights into the power of a growth mindset and how it influences success.

3. **"Grit: The Power of Passion and Perseverance" by Angela Duckworth**
    - Examines the role of grit and perseverance in achieving long-term goals.

4. **"The Lean Startup: How Today's Entrepreneurs Use Continuous Innovation to Create Radically Successful Businesses" by Eric Ries**
    - Provides a framework for innovation and entrepreneurial success.

5. **"The 7 Habits of Highly Effective People: Powerful Lessons in Personal Change" by Stephen R. Covey**
    - A classic guide to personal and professional effectiveness through seven key habits.

6. **"Daring Greatly: How the Courage to Be Vulnerable Transforms the Way We Live, Love, Parent, and Lead" by Brené Brown**
    - Focuses on the importance of vulnerability and courage in personal and professional life.

Appendix B: Worksheets and Templates

This section includes printable versions of the worksheets and templates referenced in the chapters. These tools are designed to help you implement the strategies discussed and track your progress effectively.

1. Goal Setting Worksheet

Purpose: To help you set and track your personal and professional goals.

Instructions:

- Define your short-term and long-term goals.
- Break them down into actionable steps.
- Set deadlines and milestones.
- Track your progress and adjust as needed.

2. Time Management Template

Purpose: To organize and prioritize your tasks and responsibilities.

Instructions:

- List your tasks and categorize them by priority.
- Allocate specific times for each task.
- Monitor your progress and adjust your schedule as necessary.

3. Resilience Journal

Purpose: To reflect on challenges and your responses to them, and to track your development of resilience.

Instructions:

- Record recent challenges and how you addressed them.
- Reflect on your emotional responses and the lessons learned.
- Identify strategies that worked and areas for improvement.

4. Positive Reframing Exercise

Purpose: To practice reframing negative situations into positive opportunities.

Instructions:

- Write down recent negative situations or thoughts.
- Reframe them by exploring potential positive outcomes and alternative perspectives.
- Reflect on how this shift in perspective impacts your mindset and actions.

5. Adaptability Practice Plan

Purpose: To develop and strengthen your adaptability skills.

Instructions:

- Identify areas where you want to become more adaptable.
- Set specific goals for trying new experiences or changes.
- Track your experiences and reflect on your growth in adaptability.

These resources and tools are intended to support your ongoing journey of growth and success. By utilizing these materials, you can continue to develop your skills, overcome challenges, and achieve your goals effectively.

Bibliography

Here's a detailed list of books, articles, websites, and other resources that align with the themes of success, personal development, and lifelong learning covered in the book.

Books

1. **Clear, James.** *Atomic Habits: An Easy & Proven Way to Build Good Habits & Break Bad Ones*. Penguin Books, 2018.
   - An insightful guide on how to build positive habits and break negative ones through small, incremental changes.

2. **Dweck, Carol S.** *Mindset: The New Psychology of Success*. Random House, 2006.
   - Explores the concept of fixed vs. growth mindsets and their impact on personal and professional success.

3. **Duckworth, Angela.** *Grit: The Power of Passion and Perseverance*. Scribner, 2016.
   - Examines the role of grit and perseverance in achieving long-term goals and overcoming obstacles.

4. **Ries, Eric.** *The Lean Startup: How Today's Entrepreneurs Use Continuous Innovation to Create Radically Successful Businesses*. Crown Business, 2011.
   - Provides a framework for innovative business practices and entrepreneurial success through continuous learning and adaptation.

5. **Covey, Stephen R.** *The 7 Habits of Highly Effective People: Powerful Lessons in Personal Change*. Free Press, 1989.
   - A classic guide on personal and professional effectiveness through seven key habits.

6. **Brown, Brené.** *Daring Greatly: How the Courage to Be Vulnerable Transforms the Way We Live, Love, Parent, and Lead*. Gotham Books, 2012.
   - Focuses on the importance of vulnerability and courage in personal and professional life.

7. **Sinek, Simon.** *Start with Why: How Great Leaders Inspire Everyone to Take Action*. Portfolio, 2009.
   - Explores the power of purpose and why having a clear "why" is crucial for leadership and motivation.

8. **Cameron, Julia.** *The Artist's Way: A Spiritual Path to Higher Creativity*. TarcherPerigee, 1992.
   - Offers a guide to unlocking creativity and overcoming barriers to artistic expression.

9. **Heath, Chip, and Dan Heath.** *Switch: How to Change Things When Change Is Hard*. Crown Business, 2010.

- Provides strategies for effectively managing change and implementing new habits.

10. **Kabat-Zinn, Jon.** *Wherever You Go, There You Are: Mindfulness Meditation in Everyday Life.* Hyperion, 1994.
    - Introduces mindfulness meditation practices and their benefits for personal well-being.

About the Author

Vivek Pandey is an Azure Data Engineer with a passion for personal development and success strategies. With years of experience in the technology field, Vivek has worked extensively with data solutions and cloud computing, applying a keen analytical mindset to problem-solving and innovation. Alongside his professional expertise, Vivek is dedicated to helping individuals unlock their potential and achieve their aspirations.

Drawing from a rich blend of professional experience and personal insights, Vivek integrates lessons from both ancient wisdom and modern psychology. This unique perspective allows him to offer practical advice and strategies for leading a fulfilling and successful life. His journey through the world of data engineering has taught him the importance of adaptability, continuous learning, and the pursuit of meaningful goals, all of which are reflected in the guidance provided in this book.

Acknowledgments

I am deeply grateful to the many individuals who have supported and guided me throughout the creation of this book. Your encouragement, wisdom, and unwavering belief in me have been invaluable.

Family: To my family, whose love and support have been a constant source of strength. Your patience and understanding have allowed me to pursue my passions and complete this work. The values and lessons you've imparted have deeply influenced the perspectives shared in these pages.

Friends: To my friends, who have been my sounding board and cheerleaders. Your feedback, encouragement, and shared experiences have enriched this book and provided invaluable insights. I am grateful for your companionship on this journey and for helping me stay motivated and inspired.

Mentors: To my mentors, whose guidance and wisdom have been instrumental in shaping both my personal and professional growth. Your expertise and advice have helped me navigate challenges and refine my understanding of success and development. The lessons you've taught me are woven into every chapter of this book.

To all of you who have played a role in my journey, thank you for your support and belief in my vision. This book is a testament to the collective influence of those who have inspired and guided me. Your contributions have made this work possible and have been a significant part of its creation.

With heartfelt gratitude and appreciation,

Vivek Pandey.

www.ingramcontent.com/pod-product-compliance
Lightning Source LLC
Chambersburg PA
CBHW062126220526
45471CB00010B/3903